DAN AND PHIL GO OUTSIDE

Dan Howell **&** *Phil Lester*

EBURY PRESS

1 3 5 7 9 10 8 6 4 2

Ebury Press, an imprint of Ebury Publishing
20 Vauxhall Bridge Road
London SW1V 2SA

Ebury Press is part of the Penguin Random House group of companies whose addresses
can be found at global.penguinrandomhouse.com

With special thanks to Mark Forrer, Fleur Brooklin-Smith, Marianne Turton, Anna Johnstone, Matt
Kaunitz, Ed Stambollouian, Chris Hewitt, Martyn Lester, Cornelia Dahlgren, Juliet Kozlow, Lauren
Koontz, Cat Valdes, Tara McMullen, Showtime Photo Booth, PhotoWorks Interactive,
istockphoto and Getty Images

Inside Design: Dave Brown at Ape. Apeinc.co.uk

Senior Commissioning Editor: Sara Cywinski

First published by Ebury Press in 2016

www.penguin.co.uk

A CIP catalogue record for this book is available from the British Library

ISBN 9781785035227

Printed and bound by Firmengruppe APPL, aprinta druck, Wemding, Germany

INTRODUCTION

The Amazing Tour is Not on Fire! Not the best name in my opinion.

What do you mean, Dan? It's a great name! One thing was The Amazing Book Is Not On Fire, and this was the tour. It made perfect sense.

Yeah but 'tour' was confusing. What were we touring? The book? A Q&A? Maybe it should have been 'show' or 'theatrical extravaganza that's really good and was loads of effort'.

You mean TATETRGAWLOEINOF?

Okay, fine. So we did it. Dan and Phil actually went outside.

We released our book, hopped in a car to go on tour and didn't stop until we did a lap of the world!

And, somehow, we survived to tell the story.

I think we mainly survived by ordering pancakes for breakfast at every hotel. So why did we make this, Dan?

Well, physical objects are important to me; I need something to caress, as I silently weep, pondering my regrets. So *TATINOF* definitely deserved a monument of its own.

Throughout our journey we've had so many incredible adventures, and have made so many memories with everyone, that we decided we should seal them forever in a photo book!

I mean I doubt I'll ever leave the house again after this, so we need some proof that it happened.

We've captured everything: before the tour began, all through its life, and beyond!

All the way into the afterlife, where Larry the Llama and Phil's giant lion dance with Jesus in heaven.

So drink something sugary to get you 'fricking zazzed' and open your eyes wide, as you're about to witness the tale of how Dan and Phil go outside.

Wow, was that rhyme intentional?

BEFORE THE TOUR

Life before the tour. I don't really remember what that was like...

They all feel like implanted memories that the government gave me so that I don't realise I'm actually just a robot whose sole purpose is to perform the show.

We announced the tour around March and then had (on top of all the other things) just a few months to completely create what would be TATINOF.

What did that feel like?

I'd say nervously excited, like I was about to give birth to this show but I didn't know if I'd read enough birthing manuals.

Now I have a disturbing mental image of you giving birth to a theatre.

Do you think you would mop my brow?

Definitely not. So here are some of the highlights of our time before we embarked on our voyage!

(You can definitely see the pre-nervousness in our eyes in some of these.)

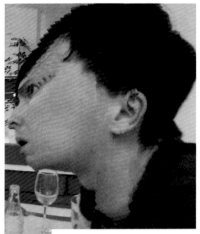

Phil in his natural state, without airbrushing.

It's a beautiful photo, Phil.

Speak to my lawyer.

We were the only Muggles in Diagon Alley that were the same size as Hagrid.

Living life on the edge.

This is why there's so many .GIFS of you falling off chairs – don't try this at home.

Relaxing, while keeping an eye on giant insects in Crete.

Lol.

Is this your revenge for the other photo?

Yes.

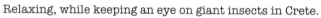

Trying out a new hairstyle.

You look particularly doge-esque in this photo.

Festive selfie with Colin.

Deck the halls with thousands of chocolatey snacks.

Me pretending to pee in the highest urinal in London!

Thanks for clarifying that you were pretending.

Recording our audiobook for *TABINOF!*

BOOKCEPTION.

Moments later he was mauled by a colossal squid!

I told you to stop watching weird anime.

UK REHEARSAL

SO, WE HAD TO MAKE A STAGE SHOW.

AND WE HAD ABOUT A MONTH!

I'm going to have a heart attack just remembering it.

How was it even possible?

It really shouldn't have been. Luckily we'd been talking about what The Dan and Phil Stage Show would be for years, so we had a heap of ideas!

Then we took those ideas and dropped them in a pile on our director, Ed, and we got a show!

Kind of, yeah.

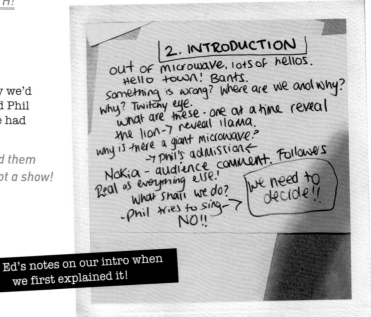

2. INTRODUCTION

Out of microwave, lots of hellos. Hello town! Bants. Something is wrong? Where are we and why? Why? Twitchy eye. What are these - one at a time reveal the lion → reveal llama. Why is there a giant microwave? → Phil's admission ← Nokia - audience comment. Followers Real as everything else! What shall we do? -Phil tries to sing → NO!!

We need to decide!!

Ed's notes on our intro when we first explained it!

Sitting with Composer Jimmy trying to think of words that rhyme with 'internet' and 'great'.

It was so cold! I actually got sick because it was so cold that we could see our breath as we talked.

It may have been freezing, with questionable lunch options and a toilet full of spiders, but it had a classic aesthetic and good reverb for writing the song, which was all we needed.

The place we all congregated and birthed *TATINOF* was, quite appropriately, an abandoned church.

Dil practising his walk through the crowds, a prophecy?

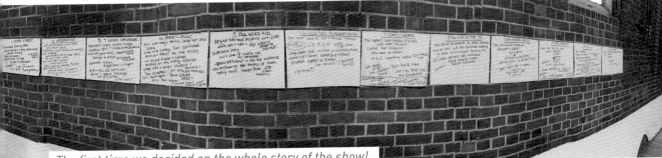

The first time we decided on the whole story of the show!

What a glorious mess all in a line. It makes perfect sense, doesn't it?

It was a strange time, as the whole show was just us walking around imagining it all, until the set and the props were made.

When we were shown little things like the llama legs, the giant question-mark cube and the magic, I got tingly feelings!

Do you remember how you felt seeing the set for the first time?

Honestly, I think I just stared, with my mouth open, for ten minutes not believing that we were responsible for something so awesome-looking.

Nadia looking snazzy in the first attempt at llama legs for Dan!

My first ever custom clothes fitting! And it was for these.

Our dance choreographer telling us to hold the hats with more pizzazz.

Dan's first ride on Larry.

After a solid month of practising the show,
non-stop all day for 10 hours, we were ready.

We packed our bags and headed up north to
Scotland for our first ever show. *TATINOF BEGAN!*

BUILDING THE SET!

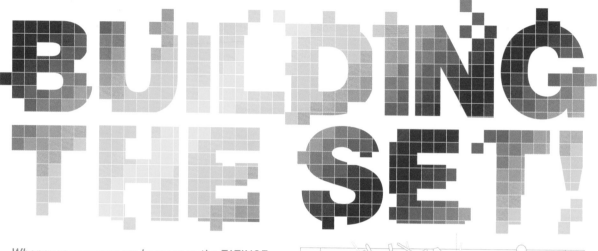

Whenever someone we know sees the TATINOF set for the first time, their mind is blown.

I mean, it is literally a giant, pixel-exploding microwave covered in images, with a giant lion and llama either side of it.

Don't forget the two houseplants!

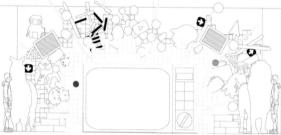

When we gave our ideas to James, the set designer, we did not appreciate just what a feat it would be to create, and how insane and incredible it would be!

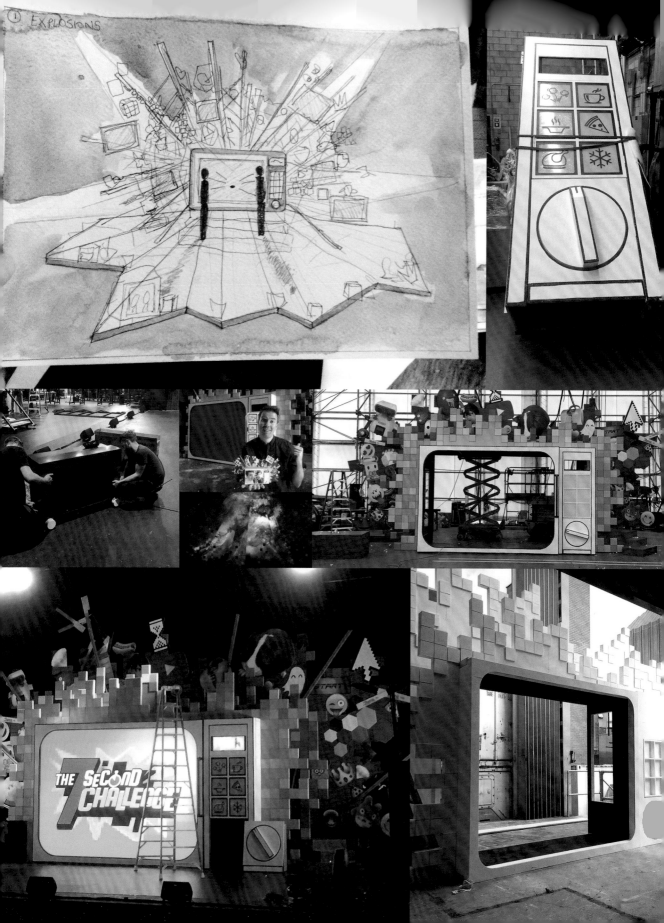

SETTING UP THE SET

Every show day, after waking up at midday and enjoying a slow laptop browse, we'd waddle into the theatre to see our set fully erected!

Did you have to say fully? Yes, as if by magic, our huge and elaborate set, with its hundreds of pieces, was all in place and ready for us to scratch.

That magic was actually our crew, who woke up at 6am every morning to stitch it together by hand, before taking it apart and shoving it in a truck again at night.

Now we know why they got through so many donuts and a lot of coffee!

PROPS

Turn Into a dolphin and swim to the other side of the room!!

THE
AMAZING

PHIL

I WENT TO #TATINOF AND ALL I GOT WAS THIS LOUSY PLATE

PHIL   DAN

ON THE ROAD-UK

Touring the UK meant a lot of driving on winding roads. Whoever built the roads in the UK was obviously trying to win the bendiest road contest.

It was a true test of my stomach! Everyone was happily using their laptops and phones, while I had my face pressed against the window for most of the journeys. My travel sickness was ridiculous!

I've never seen you so green, it was like you were trying to dethrone me from my swamp.

Thankfully, my trusty zebra neck pillow helped out a lot and I made it to every venue without throwing up on Dan.

Do you want a medal?

Kind of, yes.

Look out for animal-print neck braces on the catwalk in 2018.

We are always ahead of the trends, Danny.

Phil during one of the rare moments he wasn't quietly being sick in his mouth.

Dan regaling us with a story about a freshly discovered meme.

Despite being barf-worthy, the travel was pretty beautiful! Especially when we were going into Scotland!

I want to play the bagpipes and live in Loch Ness! It was like an ancient fairy tale, except the townspeople throw cans of Irn Bru at you and say you look like Justin Bieber.

Guess which two photos I took and which two Phil took.

Hey! It's a beautiful blur that is, in fact, a metaphor for our fast-paced journey around the world.

THEATRES

STAGE DOOR

One of the coolest things about going on tour, which we didn't even consider when we were planning it, was the amazing buildings we were able to perform in!

Now that might sound kinda lame, "Ooh, amazing building... What are you, a buildingphile?" but, seriously, some of the chandeliers were off the snazz charts.

Especially in the big cities, where the theatre was often one of the oldest buildings there, which meant that, back when people cared about theatre, they made them super opulent!

Seriously! We'd be in the middle of a place like Oakland and walk into the craziest building I'd ever seen.

Whether it's the unusual decor, questionable carpets or even the backstage area, we did feel special walking through these buildings.

It is a tradition in the theatre world to either sign the walls or spray a stencil of your show art on the corridors! There was everything from Les Mis to The Book of Mormon, and everyone from Frank Sinatra to Shrek himself signing the walls.

We should have made a *TATINOF* stencil that was just of our faces.

That sounds very obnoxious.

Exactly. Honestly, though, seeing all the people who had performed in the same venues as us really put into perspective how crazy it was that we were on this tour and how lucky we were too.

Yeah, I mean seeing the plaque that The Beatles had signed next to your dressing room would make anyone feel special!

No, I was referring specifically to the Shrek musical.

Generic marble aesthetic.

A beautiful gilded sculpture of me.

Again, we use our height to our advantage!

Philadelphia had a 'ghost light', which they say they keep on to ward off the spirits that haunt the theatre!

I thought, 'Wow! Really? That's a waste of energy!' until they pointed out that it also stops people from walking off the stage if they are working at night.

I could have used that in Florida...

Bow down to King Lester!

The terrifying dystopian AU none of us want to live in.

SHOW DAY

IT'S SHOW DAY.

The day begins waking up on the bus, freshly
shaken from a night of not hitting deer.

*We slam a couple of bowls of the good sugary stuff and strut
into the theatre like we're temporarily renting the place.*

We mark our territory in the dressing room and stride
confidently on to the stage, where we check our sound
(in what is commonly referred to as 'sound check').

*We then have our team of surgeons carefully apply
our 'interaction faces' and proceed to the meet up.*

After mingling with the peasantry, we decide whose
fates we will seal on the stage by choosing the
challenges, crafts, Weird Kid stories and questions
found by the crew.

*Next, cement is mixed with Earth's finest sand
and carefully scraped around our faces to
form our stage makeup.*

Then we get the microphones inserted
into us like puppets.

*And it's show time! We strut out
with a swagger and do our thang.*

34

The time we watched *Game of Thrones* on our giant microwave screen using the theatre speakers.

Now that's a home cinema!

"Please put that down immediately."

A Weird Kid preparing to be inserted into the 'window of shame'.

Happy birthday to the Meme Queen.

Looks like our sound guy, Chris, hit the spot!

That's the face I make when he puts his freezing hands up my back. No consent.

Phil deciding what humiliating form of suffering he will publicly subject me to in the 7 Second Challenge.

I wonder what that mum was asking Dan.

Hey, how do you know she's a mum? Might just be an older follower, if you know what I'm saying.

Dan, stop winking.

A question being recorded for 'Uncle Dan's Phone Support Hotline'!

Wait, is that?

Yup. Didn't use it in the show, funnily enough.

MEETING OUR AUDIENCE

Of course, TATINOF was about the actual stage show, but another really important part was meeting our audience!

We'd literally not be writing this for any reason if no one watched our videos in the first place. So, uh, thanks?

Internet audiences are weird because, even though you see that you have however many followers on a website, it's hard to think that they are all individual people! When a video has views, that is a real person that has actually sat down and watched what we've made. I kind of don't understand that part.

It's surreal, as there are very few moments that actually make what we do seem 'real'. YouTube is very 'in your head', as you are imagining an audience out there laughing and commenting, but because you don't actually see the real people emoting, it just stays in your head. That can be kind of hard sometimes, as I tell you now the positive reinforcement of a million people laughing would probably be really helpful. That's why we love it so much whenever we do a show or go to a convention and get to meet our audience!

Hearing the stories people have to tell us about who they are, how they discovered our videos and how it made them feel is my favourite thing about being an 'entertainer'! I love that I started on YouTube as someone just wanting to join a community of weirdos talking to each other in videos, but by keeping it going as a creative hobby that I love, my 'job' is something that makes people happy!

Totally. Until I met my followers for the first time, YouTube was just fun. It was a creative expression, a game and a challenge to put myself out there and attempt to write funny videos. But when the first person to tell me that just watching these videos, which I had made, actually made them happy, it made what I do seem so much more valuable. After all, I often think that everything I make is trash and contemplate all the billions of people out there who agree, but if one person watching said trash enjoys it, then what other validation do I need? Well, a lot, but it's a great start!

Another thing that I love is seeing how diverse our audience is. While it's mostly young people, we see a lot of parents, older siblings, children and even a couple of animals!

That dog has been the highlight of my entire life so far. You're right though, the colours of TATINOF are really everything in the spectrum of light, never mind the rainbow. I think what it shows is that no matter your age, body, gender, sexuality, taste in music or opinions on whether or not the existence of anime is a crime against humanity that needs to be destroyed at all costs, you are all welcome to have a great time!

Seriously, though, getting into anime destroyed our productivity.

The moment of the meeting is quite funny and weird. Having done every event ever, and experiencing the best and worst ways of organising things ever, we thought it'd be nice to let people mingle in a room to chat, snack and listen to some music before we arrive.

Don't get Dan started on the VIP playlist.

Ah, yes, the other playlist! See I had much more freedom when it came to energy levels and artists with this one–

–Dan, please.

Sorry.

We even left a guest book for people to sign, some of which we will include later on!

One of the coolest things we heard was that *TATINOF* was an opportunity for people to meet friends they'd had online for years. When I was a teen on the internet (5 billion years ago, haha kill me), websites like Twitter and Tumblr, which made it super easy for fandoms or just people that shared the same interest to converse en masse, didn't really exist, so I never had the internet friends that I so sorely needed back then!

Seriously, Dan had no friends.

Thanks. But, really, Phil and I being the connection that causes people to have a community or a friendship group that they can count on for laughs, companionship or just procrastination is something I appreciate, especially as an emo who silently cried into my MCR t-shirt after people threw rocks at me.

For us, it's a period of the day where we meet over a hundred people then go on stage to perform the show, but we always need to remember that for the other people it's a single, short moment that they might have been looking forward to for ages!

Oh totally. It's completely normal to have a resting-face, or breathe, or yawn – even if you're having a great time – but we think it's so important to remember that, at that moment, we're there for them.

Usually my cheeks actually hurt from smiling for an hour, it's a great workout! How do your arms cope from holding all those phones up, Dan?

I think I have one Popeye arm from taking selfies, and one that's like a withering snake.

We try to have a unique conversation with everyone but we can't help the same things coming up.

You mean people being shocked and horrified at how obnoxiously tall we are?

Well, I wasn't going to put it like that, but yeah.

It's usually: "Dan, can you take the selfie? You have noodle arms." "Wow, this is as awkward as I thought it'd be!". And, "Sorry for stepping on your foot."

Don't forget the "You smell nice!"

That is true! People, it is important to smell nice, especially on days when you plan to hug hundreds of people.

I think Dan may be one of the best selfie takers of all time.

It's possible. I don't take selfies of myself that often (don't go outside, y'know), but the sheer amount of training I have accomplished on this tour means that I think I may be in the top one per cent of photo takers, alongside the Kardashians and the NSA.

*People always ask why Dan takes all the photos...
I just don't know how to hold the phone.*

Honestly, I have tried to train him, guys, but you don't understand. I say, "Hey, you put your middle finger and ring finger behind the phone, and then hold it steady with your forefinger and little finger, leaving your thumb free to focus and press the photo button!" What proceeds is like watching Quasimodo trying to break an egg on a rock.

You're an octopus, Dan, no one can do that. You're a freak of nature!

Well, there's phone-holding ability, then there's the dropping.

I can't believe you brought this up! Okay, fine. In the UK, someone specifically asked if I could take the selfie, so I obliged, tried to do the weird claw hand thing – and I dropped the phone.

You smashed the phone. You caused an actual screen crack on a shiny new phone.

I felt so bad! The person seemed to laugh and said, "That's so Phil," but I don't think they quite realised what I did. I dropped their baby!

And that, everybody, is why nobody lets Phil hold their actual babies.

Posing is another beast in its own right.

"Nah I don't want a selfie, can we do a pose?" No other words strike as much fear into my heart. What will it be? Charlie's Angels? Awkward Prom photo? High School Musical jumping? I'm just afraid to get it wrong!

When I first experienced this I was like, okay you want me to do this very specific thing? Do you know that I'm comfortable with this? I mean, I am, but do you think I'm just a doll for you to pose and objectify?! Then I thought, eh, who cares? I'm just standing in a certain way and making people laugh hysterically, so get over it. Ergo – I LOVE THE POSING, BRING IT ON!

Some of my favourites include the 'Sailor Moon Pose', dabbing and the girl that stood on our knees.

In the UK, a critical issue for the production of the tour quickly became the amounts of gifts people were giving us.

Now, when we say gifts, we don't mean in a gross way, like people were bestowing us with Gold, Frankincense and Myrrh, we mean just letters, drawings and the odd snack.

Mountains of chocolate, Phil. They nearly had to wheel us onto the stage in London.

After we'd read the letters, we actually had to buy a storage unit to keep them safe, as there is no storage in our apartment!

It was all under my bed at one point, and I was literally sleeping on your kind words!

Yep. That sounds weird.

I understand why, though. People wanted to tell us their story in a longer way than they wanted to say in front of people. Maybe they saw something on their travels and thought of us, or just wanted to make sure we were eating so forced us to consume toffee in front of them.

What can we say? We have such a kind and generous audience! Well, maybe not all the people that gave Dan whisks, but still.

Emotionally, though, it is a strange experience, as it can vary a lot! Someone will come who's super hyper and excited, then the next person might have something serious and sincere to say, then someone who's just super chill and sarcastic, then someone who wants you to twerk while their mum takes a burst.

Thank you for visiting SEATTLE!

Sometimes I actually get quite emotional hearing the stories people say. It may be whatever issue in their life – an illness, family or school troubles or coming out – but either through making friends in our community or just laughing at our videos, they said it's helped them to feel happier!

That is the number one thing for me. I'm constantly questioning the meaning of existence and what I'm doing with my life, but to hear that no matter what I or anyone thinks, what I do is making people happy in some way, it's what keeps me going! Well, that and all the chocolate I'm given.

When Dan's light up shoes could be seen by everyone in the room.

Phil not understanding how plastic vampire teeth work.

Watch as Dan – Master of Selfies – takes dozens of photos with the exact same pose and face!

Hey! It works. So what is this? Photoception?

It's a thing of beauty...

and a bit creepy.

47

DRESSING ROOMS

What an emotional rollercoaster.

The moment of walking into a room and seeing where you will spend the next 12 hours is very important. What will you be given? A palace? A dank basement? We held our breath every time.

I don't know what kind of rock star vision people imagine, but as we did a 'good' show that we wanted to be in 'theatres' that had 'character', this meant we took a risk on the backstage areas.

DAN & PHIL

Yes, it turned out that the more beautiful and historical the theatre was, the more likely the backstage area was last updated in 1923.

What were your essentials?

As long as it had a sofa to nap on and power plugs within reach, everything was fine.

For me it was the lightbulb mirrors! I tell you no matter how little self-worth you think you have, sit in front of one of those babies and you'll feel like a star. Or just very warm, as those bulbs emit a lot of heat.

We laughed, we cried, we napped, we answered emails and ate bananas. Other than the bus, these small rooms were our home throughout this year.

I wonder why.

For some reason, Dan was reluctant to allow me to feed him some medicine when he was run down!

But which is the truth?

In this dressing room we encountered the unique problem of a toilet that wouldn't stop flushing.

It was stuck on flush all day. I think it drained the entire ocean.

The theatre in Reading, America, gave us a giant ticket and a bag of pretzels for performing a sold-out show!

STAR ★
DRESSING
ROOM

228

E. Jones
#MusicNeverStops
3-3-13
Nas/DMX
DPAC
ThankYOU

2013 2014 2015

AKA Johnny

PERFOR

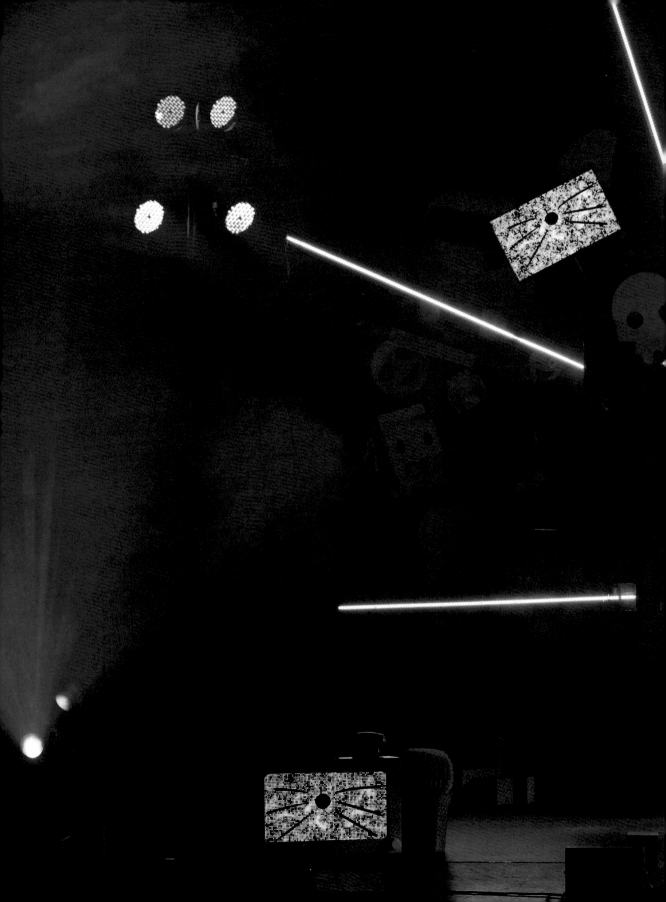

CROWDS

The energy at our shows was absolutely insane.

It started the moment we'd get the announcement, "Ladies and Gentlemen of the Amazing Tour Company, the house is now open." Like the stampede that killed Mufasa...

Wow. Really? You're just gonna drop that there?

We'd hear the earth start to shake. Dust would fall from the snazzy chandeliers and the generic noises of a zombie apocalypse would begin.

From our seats, in the dank basement dressing rooms, the earth would shake. It was kind of terrifying and very intimidating, until you took a moment to remember it's a happy earthquake/zombie apocalypse of people here to see us.

Now, something incredibly important to the success of the whole show was the playlist we put on as people took their seats:

Party In The USA – Miley Cyrus

Kiss You – One Direction

Flesh Without Blood – Grimes

The Sound – The 1975

New Americana – Halsey

Sing – Ed Sheeran

Stronger – Kanye West

Pity Party – Melanie Martinez

Like I Would – Zayn

Jealous – Nick Jonas

Hotline Bling – Drake

Youth – Troye Sivan

Victorious – Panic! at the Disco

Welcome to the Black Parade – My Chemical Romance

Breaking Free – Troy & Gabriella

Toxic – Britney Spears

Uprising – Muse

Tear in My Heart – Twenty One Pilots

She's Kinda Hot – 5 Seconds of Summer

What a masterpiece. The perfect mix of genres, trendy music, classics and straight up Dan and Phil memeage.

You spent hours reordering the playlist until it was just right! I think it changed about five times during the tour.

That's because the timing is very important. They all have to be fun, up-tempo songs to get people excited and happy, but, in the 15-to-30 minutes before the show, we have to start rolling out the bangers to get the people going. I'm talking Troye, Panic!, MCR, HSM and Toxic.

During this part of the playlist, no one backstage can even have a conversation because thousands of people are all screaming the songs at the top of their lungs.

It was truly beautiful hearing that many people sing 'Breaking Free'. Also, I totally regret putting MCR in it because all those people singing 'Black Parade' at the same time created a direct wormhole through spacetime to emo teenage Dan. I actually cried a little once.

As it got closer to show time, people would start stamping their feet, chanting, Mexican-waving, and no matter how many shows we did, my heart always started going crazy.

The moment we took our places, crouching in a giant wooden microwave ready to burst out in front of thousands of people, is something I can't describe and will never forget.

Stepping out in front of people for the first time was scary, though! I know they were all there for us, but still, so many eyes judging you from every angle.

I remember the first show, when we'd never tested out the show on a real audience before, so we were just hoping people would enjoy it – and we ended up having our expectations and eardrums completely blown out of this universe.

We were actually unsure of how it would go, as people are used to YouTubers just doing music concerts or conventions, as opposed to theatrical shows, but everyone listened, laughed and cheered exactly when we wanted them to! We had the perfect audience for our show, every single place we went in the world! I think we're very lucky to have such a smart, funny and kind crowd.

Honestly, I can relate to Gaga; the feeling I got seeing people laugh, smile and cheer at what we were doing was the best thing in the world. To know that, in that moment, no matter what was going on in our lives or theirs, we were all together having a great time and feeling happy – that was special! It made me really appreciate what we do and realise how important it can be, no matter what we or anyone else thinks.

I mean, we both probably lost half of our hearing range, but it was worth the sacrifice.

Totally.

PARTY TIME

In typical Dan and Phil fashion, we were expecting to finish our final show and slink off to a world of Mario Kart and pizza.

Ooh 'slink' – nice word. However, our crew had other plans brewing under their sneaky crew belts!

They'd only gone and booked us our own after-party! With an actual DJ and a guest list. The most people to ever turn up to one of my parties in primary school were my brother and my cousins, so this was a huge deal.

Yeah, as not just the crew but loads of our YouTuber friends came along too, which was a nice surprise! The surprise was that we had any friends, not the party thing.

My favourite part was that we got to customise our own cocktails!

Yes, the party venue agreed to create 'The Dan' and 'The Phil' for us, and we went to our own cocktail tasting session to perfect them! Yours was the sweetest and brightest thing I have ever put in my mouth.

I asked the bar women to create the sweetest cocktail known to humanity.

I just asked for mine to be black.

It was mysterious and bitter like your soul.

THE PHIL
*Vodka, Malibu, Blue curaçao,
Pineapple juice, Lemonade,
and a toasted marshmallow*

THE DAN
Patrón Cafe, Espresso, Vanilla

We 'partied' into the early hours and fortunately (or unfortunately for some people) we had a Dan and Phil photo booth to capture the action! Here are some of our favourites:

BETWEEN TOURS

After the UK tour, we went into hibernation.

You mean an actual coma?

It was weird going back to normal life! I'd wake up halfway through a dream and start singing in my bed.

I was wondering what you were doing in there.

I guess I missed the glitz and the glamour of sitting in a van for five hours on my way to a Travelodge.

Those were the days.

Here's how we spent some rare and confusing time off!

Phil got addicted to Fallout 4 and didn't move for a whole week.

Nothing gets you ready for a tour like exploring a post apocalyptic wasteland.

I tried on Dan's potato sack to prove how terrible it looks!

Rude. I think you look quite swaggy.

I look like I'm looking for my pitchfork before I tend to my lambs.

Dan took his browsing position to a whole new level.

A rare Daniel, crawling out of his burrow in the search of a snack.

Filming for YouTube Rewind in an oversized chair, while dressed as babies in a graveyard at midnight.

Typical Thursday TBH!

Dan's average face during a heated round of Mario Kart.

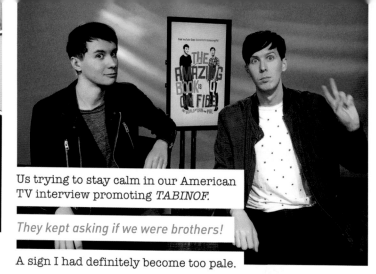

Us trying to stay calm in our American TV interview promoting *TABINOF*.

They kept asking if we were brothers!

A sign I had definitely become too pale.

Wild nerds in their natural habitat.

KILL THE IMPOSTER

Mountain climbing with my bro! My ears almost fell off.

My 90-year-old grandad kicking some serious gaming butt!

I'm not sure if we are related?

'Hawaiian'-themed Christmas party with our team. I think I nailed the Christmas/tropical vibe.

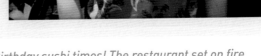

We were the only ones who turned up in costume!

They will be getting a lump of volcanic coal from Hawaiian Santa.

Who needs a headrest when you can have a Colin?

Birthday sushi times! The restaurant set on fire just before we arrived, but it was still a great night.

*Then we hosted the online stream of
the Brit Awards for the third time!*

Sadly no Kanye this year.

I went to Sri Lanka, which was a harrowing experience.

What?!

Literally no Wi-Fi anywhere. That is the last time I leave the house before researching in advance. I absorbed some big vitamin D's though! Here's me sitting on a sunbed with a dog underneath it.

We then had the mammoth task–

–Do you mean tusk?

What? No, task. We had the big task of organising the American and Australian Tours!

Oh yeah! Yeah, trying to convince a bunch of theatres around the world to book The Amazing Tour is Not on Fire by 'danisnotonfire' and 'AmazingPhil' was not easy.

Just in case anyone thinks YouTube and the internet is mainstream already, all the trails have been blazed and frontiers conquered, try organising a theatre tour.

People were like, "The Amazing who?! Is that a magician?" and I was like, "Well, technically, I do magic in the show."

You see why this was hard. They'd say, "We have *CATS* next week! *CATS*! Who are you?! No!" It is a miracle that we managed to take *TATINOF* off our little island.

We won't bore you with so many details that your brain turns into a goopy paste and dribbles out of your ears, but it turns out tours are hard to organise.

And so, after a brief rest and snacking period, we we're on the road again, only this time TO AMERICA!

USA REHEARSALS

Time for things to get big!

And not just me and Dan due to all the BBQ and burgers on the horizon!

We had to prepare for America. We knew we wanted to change a few jokes and references in the show–

–Like swapping out Queen Elizabeth for Beyoncé!

Naturally! However, we also saw it as an opportunity to improve the entire show for the final performance at the Dolby, where we'd film it.

So, just like last time, we spent a month locked in a slightly warmer and less religious room, and lived TATINOF for 10 hours a day.

A strange man squirted purple goo into our ears, and not in an erotic, alien-abduction way!

We were having special earplugs fitted that would only block out certain frequencies! Cool, right?

Yeah! However, the one time we wore them on stage, they were so good that we couldn't understand if the audience were cheering or booing during the 7 Second Challenge, so we threw them on the floor.

BY FAR the most exciting change about TATINOF USA was the jackets.

Now there was nothing wrong with our golden, shiny ones from the UK, but we just thought it was such a great opportunity to really embrace the freedom.

We regret nothing!

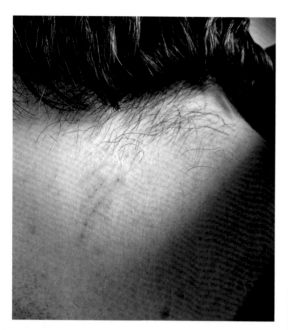

Don't let anyone tell you that we don't suffer for our art.

Our American flag bow ties and jackets were covered in so many sequins that they literally cut our necks open. The 'sequin-softening' afternoon was a good one.

Then there were the canes.

Oh my god, our poor hands! Yes, the 'magically appearing canes', from the magic part at the end of the show make it very easy to accidentally slice open your whole hand. I think we got through about 10 plasters in the first week.

The time we whacked out a map in a diner and suddenly realised what the heck we'd committed ourselves to with the USA tour.

Look at that route! So much sense.

Just give me a 'Kanye Zest' and I'll get through it.

Dan mysteriously floating like a genie.

I have come from another dimension to rid the world of weeaboos and *Minions* fans.

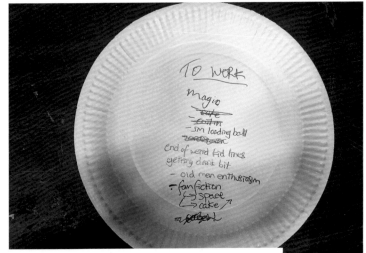

Director Ed making notes on a plate, as you do.

You don't want to know what happened before or after this photo.

My true love! I will never forget you and your sneaky probes.

???

Why are you even asking?

Dan and his big D!

Spoilers!

Our bible was *TABINOF*; the crew's was this object.

At least the dead rabbit wasn't in it when you took this.

OUR CREW

Now it wasn't just us two driving around the world on this tour!

No. We had a team of over 20 people travelling with us and even more back at home keeping it running.

Our theatre crew were the heart and soul of TATINOF.

I'd say they were also the arms, legs and all other practical muscles, as they actually did everything while we sat with a frappé being 'creative'.

True.

Honestly, when you're on the road for this long it's important that everyone gets along and has a good time (you're literally prisoners together trapped in a Dan and Phil hell-dimension), so we were so lucky to get such an awesome and talented group of people!

We'd include some more photos in here but it turns out what the crew get up to after a long day of TATINOF probably can't be published.

Our security guard, Louie, who everyone lovingly referred to as 'Drake' on the internet.

Potential cover for a mixtape he could drop at any moment.

'Straight Outta TATINOF'

Mark, the photographer who took every good photo in this book!

Fleur looking majestic, ready to ride into battle on the lion.

Who, funnily enough, is my friend from school who I grew up with! It was refreshing to have a northern accent on the bus; it made me feel back at home, or in Winterfell.

Marianne trying to avoid the paps.

Our video tech, Chris, at his battle station!

The 'Creative Team' of Jack, our lighting designer, who made us look like rock stars, even though we're two gangly dorks; James, the set designer, who made the most awesome mind-blowing stage of all time; and Director Ed, who is literally responsible for turning our 'good ideas' for a YouTuber stage show into the incredible experience it was.

The whole gang after our first show!

Everyone is actually wearing #TATINOF customised sunglasses we forced them to wear.

Anna preparing the bags of joy to give out like it is Christmas Eve.

Team spirit!

Greg and Nadia, who had the brave job of interacting with all of you to get the 7 Second Challenges, Weird Kids and Uncle Dan stories before every show!

Chris H, our sound guy, who coincidentally took those cool, colourful photos of the show from back there in his sound booth!

The secret power source of the crew.

Literally four boxes a day. I am so impressed.

Jimmy and Fleur busting out a piano duet in NY!

A long day? We've all been there.

THE TOUR BUS

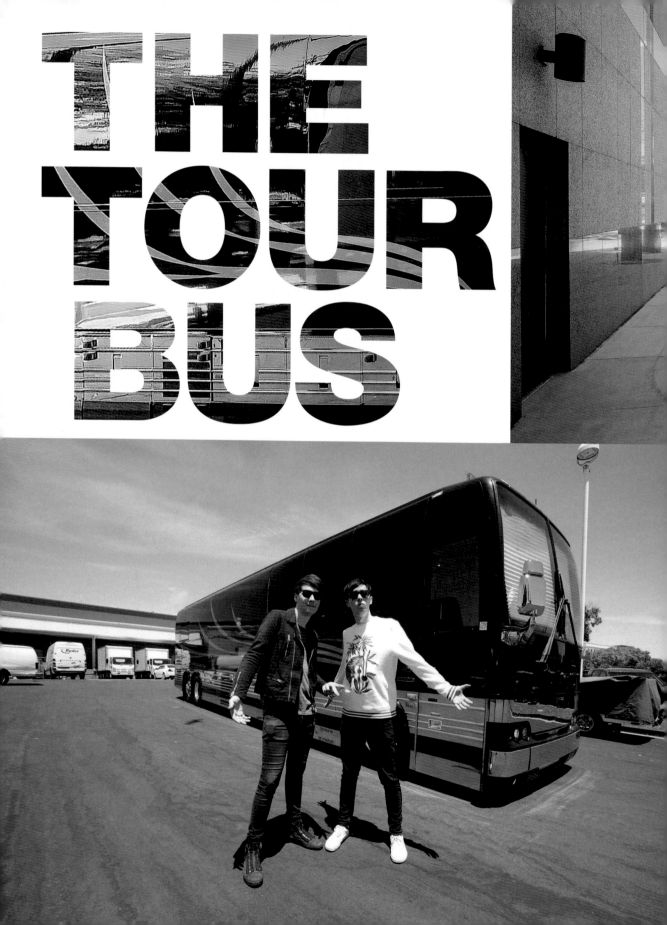

So America is big.

That is a true fact right there, Philly.

We couldn't just fly everywhere or drive during the day like we did in the UK. We needed to carry a whole load of stuff with us in the night, which meant one thing: we needed a tour bus.

We actually lived on a bus for over TWO MONTHS!

We slept, we ate, we worked, we cried – all on this bus.

It became an old friend to us, one of the gang.

Like a safe and shiny womb with wheels.

We had no idea what to expect when we were told we were getting a bus! I was expecting a dingy, dark, hell-machine, but it turned out to be a real swankfest! Apparently, the last two people to use it were my biological father, Kanye, and Ed Sheeran. I never did find any tiny orange hairs.

It had bedrooms, a fully stocked kitchen, surround-sound speakers and even a microwave for late night popcorn!

Obvs the most important feature.

There was also a shower (which we never used) and an ultra-hi-tech VHS player.

You joke, but the best two nights for you were watching *The Mummy* and *Jurassic Park* at 4am.

I can't believe how quickly we adapted to tour-bus life!

I think it helped that you had a huge bedroom all to yourself. I'm not bitter or anything.

You agreed to that rock, paper, scissors match! Plus, I think having a giant comfy bed helped a lot with my travel sickness.

Yes, that was a big concern. Things might have somehow been worse were you projectile vomiting the entire time. I'm just glad we managed to sleep on something that was moving.

It was like sleeping on a bouncy castle made of rocks. It was also pretty scary if our driver hit the brakes.

Like the 'deer incident'.

Oh yeah. One night I woke up being catapulted right out of bed! Like a giraffe being born.

Matters were made more dramatic by Phil, the eternal hoarder, keeping about 10 half-drunk coffee mugs on his bedside table that all hurled across the room and smashed in a catastrophic coffee cacophony.

I thought I was being ravaged by a poltergeist! Turns out deer were crossing the freeway and a truck flipped in an attempt to avoid them.

On the run from the law probably. I'm glad we survived!

We travelled some extremely girthy distances while we slept. I think the longest was over 1000 miles in 15 hours.

It was like teleporting; we'd go to sleep in a city and wake up extremely confused in the desert.

On the rare moments of 'day' travel, I got some good music-listening achieved! Though there's a whole lot of beautiful nothing in those middle states.

Why do Americans even need so much corn?

It's a cornspiracy!

Even though at times it felt like I was suffering from Stockholm syndrome and cabin fever all at the same time, I did miss the bus when we said goodbye!

I'm glad I gave her one last hug before we left.

Yes, I've found the line – it's you referring to the bus as 'her'!

She doesn't mind, Dan, she likes it.

This was the best seat on the bus. It had a backrest AND a table, complete with cup holders, anti-slip mat and power plugs! Many a dance-off, rap-battle and shoot-out were participated in to decide who sat here in the evenings.

Phil on his 17th coffee of the morning.

You see me browsin'.

The softest cushion on earth given to us at a show!

'I like bananas; I like bananas in the sunshine!'

Gonna sue you for copyright m8.

The best meal of the day!

So good you would sometimes eat it three times a day.

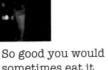

Hey, cinnamon is technically a plant!

Hey, Dan! Pose like you are eating your cereal right now.

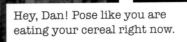

Stop ruining the magic! This is a true candid moment of Danicus Mornicus eating his natural food.

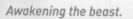

Awakening the beast.

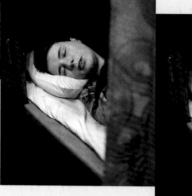

Getting my sweet revenge.

I look like I could take down a building with that almighty yawn.

The noise of you yawning is something the gods should fear.

You interrupted an amazing dream about Evan Peters and some waffles!

I don't want to know.

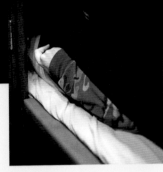

Now I'm yawning again with all this talk of yawning.

Take cover!

Me probably muting you on Twitter.

Trying to get ready in such a tiny bathroom was a challenge!

Does that explain all the toothpaste on my hair straighteners?

I hear mint is good for your follicles.

#bants

I hear throwing your toothbrush in the bin is good for your teeth!

Okay, I'll try and saliva less on your beauty products.

Just call me 'Zen Howell'.

Dan's favourite room on the bus!

Don't talk to me before I've finished my cereal.

Sushi in Texas was almost as good as sushi in Japan.

SThusklHELP ME

The exact moment of brain-freeze.

Ha! I finally caught you sleeping.

What a graceful hippo-like creature I am.

The moment of primal terror in everyone's eyes when Phil volunteered to open a bottle with a popping cork.

Everyone should have had total faith in me!

Moments later we hit a speedbump and Phil spilled his drink all over his crotch.

Nothing worse than a fizzy crotch!

One of our final nights all together!

Wait, why are you wearing my socks?

The laundry got sparse towards the end. I was desperate.

New profile pic, Dan?

I will not tolerate this bullying in my own book.

Counting down the days on the calendar somehow made it seem a bit prisoney.

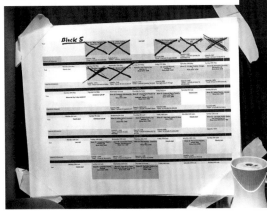

We should have scratched the days on the walls and exclusively exited the bus by squeezing through a window covered in butter!

All the camera equipment from our documentary didn't make the seats more comfortable.

The VHS next to my bed rattled so much as I tried to sleep that I stuffed it with socks.

I chose a pillow as my security object, as Dan lovingly embraces a tripod.

FLORIDA

Conveniently, my family went on holiday to Florida right before we went to rehearse for the tour, so I got to go relax before the start!

Yes. How 'convenient'!

We went for a walk and look who I stumbled across: THE SQUIRREL. This is the exact squirrel that infamously bit me last time I went to Florida!

GATORLAND

One place I had to take Dan was Florida's premiere family owned Alligator-themed theme-park. GATORLAND!

It was actually a lot cooler and safer than I thought it'd be based on that description.

I got more than I consented to when I fed this goat.

I photographed it, Phil, and my conscience isn't any cleaner.

OMGATORS

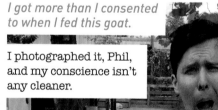

This bird was the single scariest creature I'd ever seen in my life.

It kept stalking people and pecking them!

I feel like this image is a metaphor for me and Dan.

And, of course, in their gift shop I bought my iconic bedazzled Gatorland hat!

I'm disturbed by how much it suits you.

MINI GOLF

GOLFBOYS

What do you reckon we got arrested for?

Just being too damn good at golf.

More like for hitting 20 balls into the lake.

AIR BOAT

We went on an airboat to experience true Floridian culture!

Turns out it's mostly gnats and dangerous reptiles.

Dan desperately swatting away flies!

There were so many hitting me in the face, Phil. Every hole. Every hole.

I'm not sure what this was in the gift shop, or whether it's legal in the world of science, but we had to get a photo!

It has a nice pastel aesthetic with that hat.

snek

Busted!

A turtle with one leg who kept swimming in circles. Apparently it fended off an alligator that tried to eat it. Metal.

Phil vs. Wildlife, Episode 1: The Rejection Duck

PIER

Phil vs. Wildlife, Episode 2: The Angry Pelican

NEW YORK CITY

We literally performed a sold-out show on Broadway!

That's a weird sentence to comprehend, isn't it? It's fun to go to NYC as a tourist, but it felt even more magical being there to perform a show!

As we were driving into Times Square, our bus driver started playing 'New York, New York' by Frank Sinatra!

It was like being in a movie, except my knees hurt slightly because we were kneeling at the front of our bus.

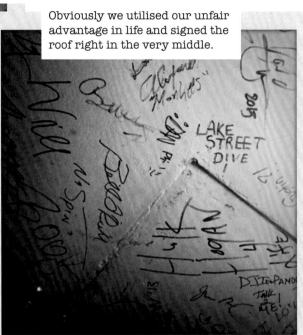

The Beacon Theatre had an elevator that had been signed by everyone who had performed there!

Obviously we utilised our unfair advantage in life and signed the roof right in the very middle.

We also managed to catch up with some internet pals at the YouTube 'Creator Summit' that happened that weekend!

Recreating *Geri's Game* at the Chess Club.

I feel like we'll both end up angrily chessing each other there in the future.

Phil being confronted with his worst fear.

Their heads are so long!!

Going for a walk and doing some filming with Director Ed!

BOSTON

Boston was where I had the best pizza of my entire life.

Bit of a random way to introduce this?

That's the most important thing there is to say!
Soy sauce on a pizza, try it.

We did have a lovely morning roaming the Common!

And that was just two days before Justin Bieber
infamously walked around with no socks on...
to think our paths could have crossed.

I'd have donated a pair of foxes and sloths to him.

*Dan attempting to look deep in thought while
looking at the lake. A squirrel ruins the photoshoot.*

Phil vs. Wildlife, Episode 3: The Pigeon Problem

Aesthetic selfies, apparently not exclusive to Japan!

Behind-the-selfie

SHIBE ALERT DROP EVERYTHING.

Never say that again.

They didn't want the P!

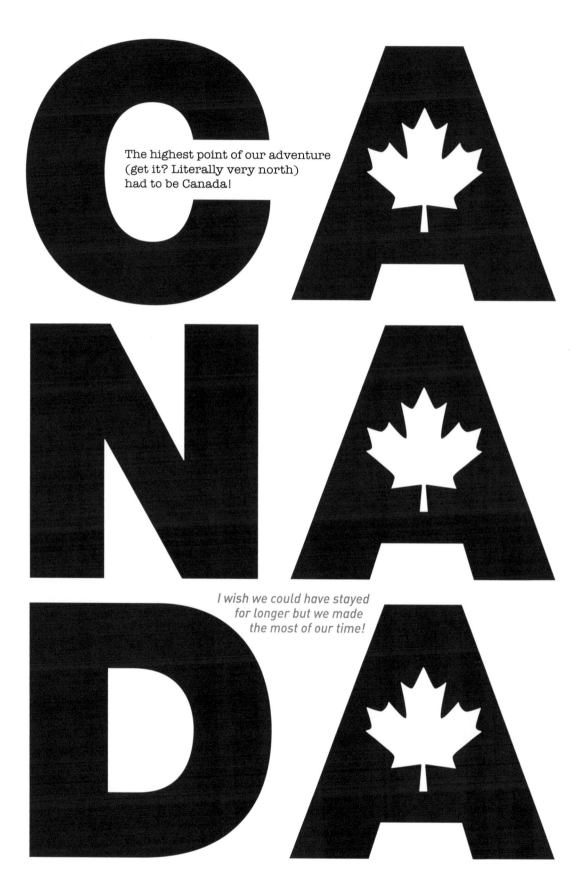

The highest point of our adventure (get it? Literally very north) had to be Canada!

I wish we could have stayed for longer but we made the most of our time!

This is me having successfully crossed the border into Canada!

I was expecting a ranger on the back of a moose to check our passports so I was kinda disappointed.

WTF is that?

IDK. I figured it was the Canadian Stonehenge or something?

It's creepy AF.

We made friends with Michael the Canadian moose.

I'm pretty sure we weren't meant to hug him, he's like the Obama of Canada.

NIAGARA FALLS

We didn't even realise we could go to the falls until we drove past it and went "OMG PULL OVER WATERFALL QUEST RIGHT NOW"!

Phil vs. Poncho

Phil had some issues putting his poncho on. It took him about 25 minutes.

Adult Voyage to the Falls

HORNBLOWER NIAGARA CRUISES

Boats Depart Every 30 Minutes in Season

Node26 Receipt:3190
5/6/2016

SEE REVERSE FOR
TERMS & CONDITIONS

0026080520161246231635

Adult

Boats Depart Every 30 Minutes

Node26 Receipt:3190
5/6/2016

SEE REVERSE FOR
TERMS & CONDITIONS

A

A

It is honestly one of the most incredible things I have ever seen! IT WAS SO BIG?!

Well, it is a wonder of the world Phil.

It was one of the moistest experiences of my life.

TMI, Phil.

125

TORONTO

Our day at the big game.
Was it a big game? I have no idea.

LET'S GO BLUE JAYS!

THIS IS YOUR TICKET

8825 8886 3308 7390

SECTION	ROW	SEAT
516R	31	9

EVENT
Toronto Blue Jays vs. Los Angeles Dodgers
FRI MAY 06 2016 7:07 PM

Pretending I know what a sport is.

Almost a successful panorama.

I'll do it one day, without horribly warping reality.

The real reason we had a good time.

450 metres beneath that glass floor. AAaaAahhhh!

I managed to hold that smile for one second before running away squealing.

Phil, stop desecrating the monument.

I'm like Godzilla but with sexy moves.

Not Dan's best choice of place to have a crisis.

Phil managed to survive a meal at the revolving restaurant without getting motion sickness. What a hero.

PHILAD ELPHIA

Philly is in Philly!

Immediately delete that.

You're just jealous because there isn't a place called Danny.

Like every tourist, we had to spend a good hour watching people jog up and down the steps from *Rocky*! To think each of them was humming to their own imaginary little montage.

PHILLY BALBOA! I had to.

You took like 10 minutes walking up and panting.

One other important quest while we were there was to find the legendary 'Philly Cheesesteak'!

I wasn't sold based on the name, but I felt it was culturally important.

Just before the moment of truth. How was it?

INCREDIBLE! Light on the cheese like a pizza, but it was so juicy and amazing. Thanks dude at the market for making such a sweet sub.

WASHINGTON DC

We went to go say hi to Obama!

I expected a lot more fence-age...
to say that's where he sleeps.

*There were probably secret laser beams
and alligators ready to be released if
you got closer, Dan.*

Enjoy the sight of us desecrating so many
important monuments and buildings.

Your eyes will absorb the freedom through the page!

Cheeky selfie with Abe.

How did we not get deported?

CHICAGO

I'm gonna put it out there and say that I was disappointed by the lack of wind in the so-called 'Windy City'.

What were you expecting?

The odd cow flying by the window would have been nice?

I'm burning your DVD of *Twister*.

Thankfully the city made up for its lack of wind with some swanky architecture and cartoonish water!

How to make pedestrians hate you.

Here's Phil sulking after a woman shouted at him for taking selfies in the middle of the pavement.

I can't believe how blue the river was! It was like a cartoon river.

The River Thames in London should hang its dirty polluted head in shame—

—And go have a bath.

How can a river have a bath?

Sounds like a riddle! If a river had a bath, did it make a sound?

BOAT TOUR

Because we're so cultured and mature we decided to go on an 'Architecture Boat Tour'!

I know, right! Check me out appreciating all the... fine buildings.

PC0531 300PM G1 42 A 41.64 ERC0531
00CCTX RIV CRUISE 3PM
300PM   THE OFFICIAL CHICAGO   CN 07042   300PM
CFL 13X ARCHITECTURE FOUNDATION   ADULT
G1 42   R I V E R   C R U I S E   G1
4011315 VALID THIS CRUISE ONLY!!   41.64
A31MAY6 MICHIGAN AVE @ WACKER DR. CA
         TUE MAY 31 2016   42

General Admission Seating
No Refunds or Exchanges

CHICAGO ARCHITECTURE FOUNDATION

12561551528

CHICAGO ARCHITECTURE FOUNDATION

CHICAGO ARCHITECTURE FOUNDATION RIVER CRUISE
ABOARD CHICAGO'S FIRST LADY CRUISES

"TOP TOUR IN CHICAGO!
ONE OF THE TOP 10 TOURS IN THE U.S."
—TRIPADVISOR USERS

CHICAGO'S FIRST LADY
CHICAGO'S FINEST FLEET

You found a way to make this inappropriate.

Hey, they were truly shiny and glorious!

This was my favourite building!

So creepy. If I had a car I would definitely accidentally reverse it over one of those ledges.

That is why you don't drive cars.

So just when we got fully zazzed by the buildings, it started to rain!

It was kinda awkward because we all had to go inside the boat to stay dry, but the tour guide kept explaining the buildings, even though we couldn't see them.

Thankfully, we bought some glorious hobbit hair protection ponchos.

Made from a freshly flayed smurf!

Their sacrifice meant a lot.

The Bean

When I mentioned we were in Chicago, literally every tweet was 'GO SEE THE BEAN'!

I was kind of scared and intrigued, but it turned out it was a giant fourth-dimensional mirror-bean.

How many Dan and Phil's can you see in the Chicago Bean?

Truly beantacular.

It also created the opportunity for some dank reflection selfies.

It turned out Chicago is home to the single most glorious food object I've ever experienced.

OR NOT.

THE DEEP DISH PIZZA.

It was like an entire cake made out of cheese.

A.K.A. the greatest experience of my life. I transcended to a plane of existence where all I could sense was dairy and regret.

HOUSTON SPACE CENTRE

Technically, they spell it as 'Space Center', but I refuse to submit to your sensible ways of spelling things, America.

We went to NASA!! I'd been to Kennedy Space Center in Florida, so I was pumped for this one.

Please never be 'pumped' for anything. It was incredibly cool, though! Also, it turned out that everyone who worked there was a student, so it was like a mini-convention for us. Thanks to everyone who let us cut the lines!

We went for a tour of the actual NASA campus, which was exciting!

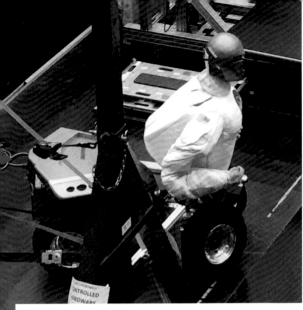

A real moon-robot with ultra-precise claw hands!

It looks like a scientist bred a human with a quad-bike. "KILL Meeee PleEASE end my SUffering!!'"

#1 on the list of vehicles Phil should never pilot.

Chris, our video technician, and I bought the same t-shirt! Space swag.

Dan deeply appreciating the history of the Saturn V.

I posted this photo on Instagram and flipped it upside down, saying I was 'having a float' in NASA's anti-gravity chamber and a lot of people believed me. Shout out to all the people who think we have that technology... never stop believing.

THE CADILLAC RANCH

Don't know what was worth singing about TBH.

Wow, Dan.

Well, the hotel receptionist did tell us not to go to the bar opposite our hotel because "people like to play with their guns in it."

True.

Anyway, something cool we heard about was an art instillation of a bunch of Cadillacs buried in the earth!

The ground was littered with spray paint cans and the idea was that anyone can come and paint/tag whatever they want. It looked awesome!

Don't mess with our gang.

Dan spent about 30 minutes spraying his magnum opus.

Is it, technically, the rarest Pepe in the entire world? I apologise for nothing.

It was very warm.

I was wearing two coatings of SPF 50.

SAN FRAN CISCO

Now San Fran was an adventure!

We had a rare 'day off'.

What's that? A sandwich?

So we hopped in a cab and decided to do everything from seal watching to street viewing to wood delving!

We voyaged to the pier in hopes of finding some top seal-age.

We managed to pose and look cool for about 4 seconds before we froze to death.

Where did that wind come from? Nearly blew my nipples clean off.

Dan found his people!

I have never felt weirder or more outcast than when I stepped into that left-handed store. We don't need our own oven gloves?!

Mildly inappropriate Alcatraz merch?

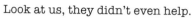

We invested in these snazzy San Fran tourist jackets to shield us from the Arctic blast.

Look at us, they didn't even help.

We had to stop for a caricature!

To be honest, he gave me a jaw line, so I'm not complaining.

They were everything we hoped they'd be.

Truly majestic creatures. They can galumph straight into my heart.

MUIR WOODS NATIONAL MONUMENT
NATIONAL PARK SERVICE DEPARTMENT OF INTERIOR

We hopped in a cab and somehow convinced the driver to
take us all the way to the woods across the bridge and back.

He was the nicest guy ever!
Maybe not the best driver, though.

No, I literally accepted death about four times driving down
the cliff path to the woods. At least he waited in the car for us!

These are the mysterious Muir Woods, known
for having some of the world's tallest trees...

And the angry chimp civilisation from the *Planet of The Apes* reboot!

We unfortunately didn't see any hyper-intelligent apes.

We did spot this deer, though!

These are the two worst photos in this book.

And this super cute chipmunk!

GRRAaargh... just looking at it makes me want it to stick it in my mouth and punch something.

Wow. Something actually taller than us!

Hiding from the Nazgûl.

Phil soiling the spirit of the woods.

Hey! I'm majestic.

Underneath-the-selfie

My bear dad.

Much scenic. Very valley. Much tree. Wow.

What even happened here?

Universe briefly imploded I think.

We were then racing against the clock to get to the Golden Gate Bridge for the sunset!

We ended up driving into some abandoned military base and hopping over a fence to get a good view.

AND WHAT A VIEW IT WAS!

We then drove up to the highest point in the city to soak in one last view!

San Fran definitely wins the awards for coolest-looking and least-fun-to-park-a-car-in city.

Then, after a two-hour drive to our next hotel, we bid farewell to our driver.

He stuck with us the whole day! His family probably thought we kidnapped him.

We had to get a photo with him after our adventure. What a dude.

VISITING INSTAGRAM!

So Zuckerberg pinged me a DM and asked if we wanted a tour of his crib.

Lying is bad.

Okay, the lovely peeps of Instagram offered to take us on a tour of their campus that they share with Facebook! When they mentioned there was free food, it was an instant yes.

Nine restaurants of free food to be precise.

We never wanted to leave.

For some reason there was a car in the Instagram office.

And Phil took the wheel! I was scared to even pretend.

It had no wheels but I still could have killed someone.

This is where Facebook plots their world domination.

It was like *Minority Report* but with much taller actors!

Tom Cruise just unsubscribed.

A literal Facebook wall! How meta.

We defaced it with our unworthy names.

A typical Facebook office.

Definitely an artificially intelligent war machine.

Shh, they are still listening.

SEATTLE

Seattle was one of my fav places. It just had an unexplainable vibe that satisfied me.

Like stroking a cat's fur in the right direction.

Yes.

Or pressing a clean toe into a fresh lump of sand.

I guess?

Or–

–Let's quit while we're ahead.

The trees in Seattle were 👌

You can't just bang out an emoji 170 pages into this book!

It's the only way I could explain my feelings about these very damp aesthetic trees.

Okay, they were pretty sexy.

Ah, so you poo on my emoji and then reveal yourself as a dendrophile? I'm not even surprised.

THE SPACE NEEDLE

I was expecting Mulder and Scully to be investigating this observation tower. It's so alien-like and mysterious.

It had that real, old-as-heck retro futurist vibe.
Now I suppose you are expecting a passage about
the journey to the top and the wonderful view?

Alas no.

They were too busy and wouldn't let us in!
Always check the website before you travel folks.

😥

Okay, that's your one emoji used up for the book.

It's like a metal Kinder Surprise with a Phil inside.

That would be disappointing.

THE WORLD'S FIRST STARBUCKS!

We completed our internal white-girl pilgrimage and visited the first ever Starbucks!

I actually stroked the window and silently cried. So much caffeine and sugar has run through my veins thanks to this building.

I'm just gonna say it, the mermaid has visible nipples.

Are we allowed to publish cartoon mermaid nipples in this book?

LET'S FIND OUT.

Free the mermaid nipple!

This session went on for about an hour before we found an acceptable one.

VEGAS

Dan and Phil RETURNED TO VEGAS!

Yeah! This wasn't originally our plan, but we added it as a last-minute date that meant we were conveniently in Vegas for my birthday.

Yes. How convenient.

Honestly, it was kind of the FBI to let us return after what happened last time.

I know! At least we managed to get through this visit without having to run away with the Cirque.

Good times.

Phil literally bathing in sun cream.

I couldn't risk a *puts sunglasses on* Phil IS on fire situation!

Literally jump out of this book right now and banish yourself.

We went up the fake Eiffel Tower to get a drink with a view!

Phil immediately proceeded to get French toast cream on his wrist.

Dan encountered his nemesis, a MIST MACHINE.

I was once trapped in a theme park ride queue with one of these for an hour. It was not a pretty sight.

A black bedazzled fedora to go with my Gatorland cap!

You have to destroy this immediately.

M'Vegas *tip*.

Then it was MY BIRTHDAY! Let us take a moment to appreciate the wrapping on a gift I was given on the tour bus.

But then, when we went into the theatre...

Witness the moment of glory when Dan was presented with a LLAMACORN PIÑATA.

It was the single most beautiful thing I'd ever seen. I could not bring myself to violently destroy it and guzzle its innards.

Phil defiling yet another helpless animal.

And then there was this.

Then, hilariously, we asked the theatre to order us a car to take us back to our hotel and look what they sent us.

A limo. How embarrassing!

I bet they thought they were doing something nice for your birthday, but OMG.

Mortifying.

Getting into a limo and gliding past all our followers is really, really not Dan and Phil style.

What did you wish for?

The cake to magically replenish itself with each bite.

Then it was time to HIT THE TOWN!

With my Llamacorn Piñata, which I still had. Surprisingly, in Vegas no one questioned a thing!

We went to go see a water acrobatics show, which was fun!

TATINOF had better musical numbers and set pieces – just saying.

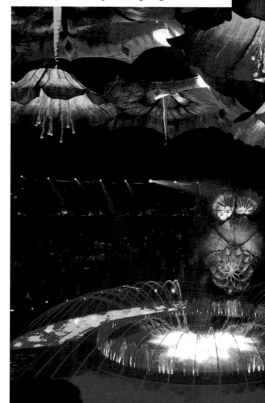

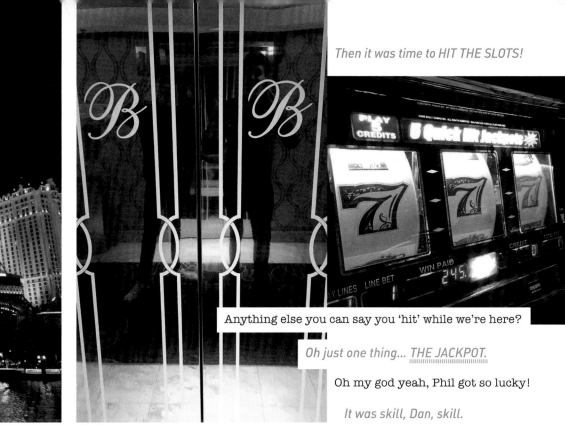

Then it was time to HIT THE SLOTS!

Anything else you can say you 'hit' while we're here?

Oh just one thing... THE JACKPOT.

Oh my god yeah, Phil got so lucky!

It was skill, Dan, skill.

So here's what happened. After blowing my life savings on an incredibly fun *Game of Thrones* slot machine, I convinced Phil to put $2 (that's seriously all) into a *Gremlins* branded machine.

Hey, it's one of my favourite movies! So I slid in two Georges and hit spin.

Now this *Gremlins* machine was a four by five grid of slots that could line up. On Phil's first spin, every single slot in the grid lined up with the same image.

Phil's actual face when this happened.

I couldn't believe it!

A crowd gathered as the machine started blaring alarms with cackling Gremlin's flying all over the screen and the winnings counter just kept going up and up.

Get this right, from $2 I won $550!!

Everyone hates you, Phil.

So, I then did what any sensible person would do, I bought a $100 chip, went up to a roulette table and put it all on red.

This is obviously the worst idea ever, so our entire group was pre-cringing ready for the night to end on a flop. We were all terrified!

The grumpy lady span that wheel and we watched it bounce and skip across the number, it teetered on the edge of black and green and with its final ounce of momentum... BAM. Red!

We were honestly so relieved that none of us even cheered, we just though 'thank god' and GTFO of there as fast as we could.

As for what happened the rest of that night, Dan...

What happens in Vegas stays in Vegas!

STEAMING

Here I present an incriminating selection of Dan 'steaming'.

What? It is steaming! Our vocal coach, Jimmy, instructed us that it was super-important when doing a lot of shows to keep your vocal chords moist.

Of course, Dan! Keep your 'chords' 'moist'.

That's literally it, Phil. It's just inhaling the steam from boiling water – loads of people do it.

'That', 'Phil', 'Water', 'People'?

Oh, whatever. Look, I found one of you!

Delete this incriminating image!

June 7, 2016

NASA

10287   10287

e All.

PINK   AC/DC

Paris
LAS VEGAS

EIFFEL*TOWER*
E X P E R I E N C E*

AMAZING
PICTURES

PHOTO CLAIM
TICKET

PHOTO ASSOCIATION METHOD PATENT PENDING

June 11th, 2016

EIFFELTOWER
EXPERIENCE

May 6, 2016

June 11th, 2016

DIL'S ADVENTURE

Now, who can forget the real star of the show?

Gosh it does make me nostalgic! To remember the time we birthed him in our gaming room with those bunny slippers and the clown suit pyjamas.

Maybe don't bring up the pyjamas, Phil; you know it's a sore topic.

Oops, sorry. Honestly, though, I've never felt like more of a proud dad than seeing him burst out of a door in the corner of a theatre and making the people near him collapse in terror.

From struggling to do the dishes, to magically forcing us to do them in an alternate dimension, he's our Dil!

We're so glad that Dil could take time out of his schedule and come on tour with us.

He's a pretty busy guy, what with the GF, his science career and travelling the world as an ambassador for the 'YouTube Let's Play Famous Characters Guild'.

I mean, the paperwork with EA took a long time and he was very demanding.

Oh, yeah! Well, this book isn't the place to discuss all of that. To think he wanted 200 white puppies in every dressing room. How is that possible? Where would we have stored them?

I thought it was a bit OTT when he'd order a pepperoni pizza and then make us pick all the toppings off individually – but I can relate to being picky.

Well, there was that one time he stormed out of the theatre right before he had to go on stage.

I guess it wasn't fair that he only got to say three lines with his real voice the whole time.

Also, when his giant head got stuck in the tour bus and we had to grease him out of it.

We used all the butter that was supposed to be for two months of toast for me, but I guess it had to be done!

And the crew didn't appreciate half their salary being transferred to Dil for his team of personal masseuses, but I'm sure they understood how important Dil's participation was for the art of the show.

We're just happy he could join us. Thanks, Dil!

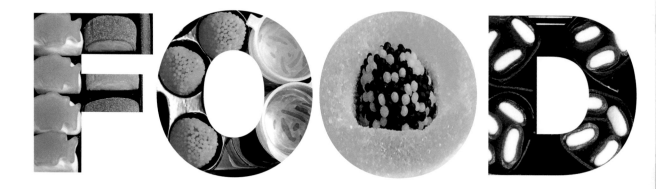

FOOD

As we all know, the most
important thing in life is food.

*What you eat, when you eat it and where are the
biggest questions in life. And we were on tour!*

This was a challenge.

*Living on the road and out of hotel rooms made it
almost impossible to cook any food, which meant
A LOT of room service and takeout. This may have
led to some slightly unhealthy choices from me...*

Slightly?

*If you offer me a kale salad or a waffle with extra
syrup and cream, what do you expect me to pick?!*

I'm not even disagreeing. It was a one-way trip
to shame land, via all the carbs in the universe,
and I don't regret a single day of it. I apologise
in advance for the lack of green on these pages.

Unless it's gummy and green, we had a lot of that.

STOP JUDGING ME, OKAY.

Coconut shrimp in our first ever meal in an actual Bubba Gump Shrimp! They played *Forest Gump* on all of the TVs.

Big Gulps, more like 'now I need to pee so bad because I drank so much liquid'.

I'm sure the marketing department is rushing to change the name as we speak.

Team burgers at Flip Burger!

Named after me, of course.

A FLIGHT OF MARGARITAS! If I still updated my Margarita blog, it would get a strong five.

My 'Key lime pie margarita' was like drinking 3 liquidised pies.

A world famous Baltimore crab cake!

How was it?

CLAWESOME!

ejector seat

Just before I realised that Cheetos are cheese flavoured! I swear they don't taste like cheese.

No cheese shaming here, Phil, despite how guilty you look.

What am I even doing?

I think these images are better left without captions.

Security guard Louie got us a 'light snack' for National Donut Day.

I just dribbled over the keyboard.

An actual cupcake-flavoured pancake from IHOP! It was more delicious than you can convey with the English language. I'd have to start making inappropriate noises.

Phil, we're categorising this as a non-fiction hardback, not erotic cooking.

Just two hunis loving life in the big city!

This photoset is a violation of my basic human rights.

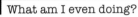

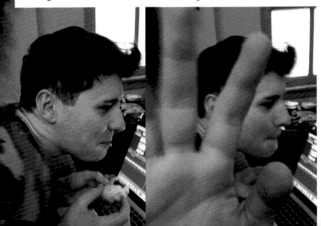

The Durham venue had an ice cream machine and it was the single best moment of my life.

Better than performing at the Dolby Theatre in Hollywood?

Do you really want the answer?

The worst day of my life.

We apologize for the inconvenience, *but the* pancake machine is temporarily out of order.

Please try our cinnamon rolls that we have set out.

Some American 'bread' with three kinds of butter and icing to dip it in!

A dangerous menu.

I went for 'butter cookie' and Phil had 'birthday cake shake'.

It had huge lumps of cake in it! It was a bit of a mistake.

Trying Buckeyes! The national candy of Ohio.

Phil's review: Pretty great!

Dan's review: A horrifying peanutty cup of regret.

Cat took us to the Griddle Cafe in LA, and they sold pancakes bigger than the entire solar system!

So much cream.

We failed.

We managed to eat about ¼ of one pancake.

I will eat this book if anyone can finish a full stack of those pancakes.

WEIRD ROOM SERVICE ENCOUNTERS WITH PHIL!

1. THE SILENT LADY

Order: *Teriyaki chicken salad and an iced coffee*

What happened: *I opened the door to a lady with black hair who was dressed head to toe in black. She delivered my salad in complete silence, with unwavering creepy eye contact! I asked how she was and she didn't respond. I gave her the money and she didn't say thank you. She just floated away out of the door. I think she was either a ghost or she was intensely scared of my fluorescent-green Muppet pyjamas. Probably the latter.*

Weirdness ranking: *3 stars*

2. FLIRTY MCFLIRTERSON

Order: *Bacon waffles and a large pot of coffee*

What happened: *A day when another human shows me any kind of romantic attention is a very rare day, but especially when I answer the door to a delivery of bacon waffles in a Buffy t-shirt and oversized Star Wars PJs. I was greeted by a middle-aged blonde lady carrying my breakfast, and I politely said, "Thank you," and she said, "Wow what a beautiful accent, it matches your face too! What strong features you have!" I stared at her in stunned silence. WHAT IS A STRONG FEATURE? Did she just sass my nose? I wasn't sure, but then she followed it up with, "Let me know if you ever need any extra syrup, if you know what I mean!" If you know what I mean!?!? NO. WHAT? I wasn't sure I wanted to know what she meant, so I just said, "Oh, hah this is a great amount of syrup for me thanks!" I closed the door. Oh dear.*

Weirdness ranking: *4 stars*

3. THE RAVE MACHINE

Order: *A large vanilla milkshake (stop judging me)*

What happened: *A teen guy arrived with my long-overdue shake and handed it to me. I made the mistake of saying "thank you", revealing my English accent, to which he started a conversation about the Mother Country! "Hey so do you live in London?" he asked. "Why, yes I do," I replied, trying to be as uninteresting as possible so I could drink my sweet, sweet milkshake. He then followed with, "So do you go to a lot of raves in England?"... A lot of raves?!?! What does someone even say to that? I was silent for slightly too long before saying, "Yeah, I don't really rave much. I mean. I'm kind of done with raving." Why am I so awkward? Why did I pretend to have ever raved? He stared at me blankly and closed the door. Remind me never to speak to another human ever again.*

Weirdness ranking: *3 stars*
(mainly due to my awkwardness, but, seriously, who uses the word rave?)

4. THE INVENTOR

Order: *Texan burger with fries and a Diet Coke*

What happened: *An old, burly cowboy delivered my burger in Texas. And, as the table was annoyingly big to push through my door, he revealed a strange springy metal contraption. He then pinned it into the hinge of the door to stop it closing! I said, "Wow, that's a cool little invention to stop the door closing! I've never seen one of those before." He pulled a sad face and replied, "I know. I invented it! I'd be a millionaire if they had let me have the patent. I definitely wouldn't be here delivering food to you. It was my life's work and it ended in ruins." WHAT DO YOU EVEN SAY TO THAT? I just replied, "Oh no! That really sucks?" I did give him a big tip out of guilt! Maybe that's his technique? He just pretends to have invented this springy thing to guilt people into tips? Either way I'm sorry for mortifying you, Mr Room Service Cowboy.*

Weirdness ranking: *4 stars*

5. THE LOUDEST SALESMAN ON EARTH

Order: *Continental breakfast*

What happened: *Before Vegas we had to get up at about 6am for the flight so I was feeling particularly delicate. I'd hung the magical room service menu on my door handle the night before and was awoken at 5:50am by the loudest knock of all time. I swear it was in the rhythm of 'We Will Rock You', but don't quote me on that. I was greeted by a tiny bald man who practically screamed in my face, "GOOD MORNING, SIR! ISN'T IT A BEAUTIFUL DAY TO BE UP THIS EARLY?" It took all my will not to reply with, "NOT WHEN YOU ARE SHOUTING IN MY FACE." I stayed politely quiet as he set up my breakfast and then he noticed my obviously snazzy NASA t-shirt. "HOW MUCH FOR YOU TO SELL THAT T-SHIRT?" he asked. I thought he was joking! I gave him a laugh. and said, "Aw, glad you like it." "NO, SERIOUSLY? I WILL GIVE YOU FREE BREAKFAST IF YOU SELL ME YOUR NASA SHIRT." Why does this happen to me? What is happening? Why is a strange man trying to buy my clothes in my bedroom at 6am? I just replied with, "Not today, sorry, but now you have a reason to go to the Space Centre hahaha," and slowly closed the door on his genuinely disappointed face. I heard him whistling the theme tune to 'A Whole New World' from Aladdin as he walked away down the corridor.*

Weirdness ranking: *5 stars*

THE MERCH TEAM!

Another gang of hooligans in the
TATINOF squad was the merch team!

Like a little appendix on the beast that hands out t-shirts.

That's the single worst mental
image I've had making this so far.

The team included my (actual) bro Martyn and Cornelia,
who were with us the whole time, which was nice!

They had their own bus, and the mammoth task of literally building a store in every theatre lobby
and lovingly laying out flower crowns to be bestowed upon people like a beautiful meadow.

Martyn said sometimes he couldn't work with the merch, as people would
queue up to take selfies with him and he couldn't get anything done!

The touch of Phil everyone. Also, Cornelia worked so
hard that I'm starting to believe her 'Swedish' identity
is actually code for 'a cyborg built to process a million
calculations a second and have cool red hair'.

They were such an awesome, kind, cool group of people who
got to interact with our audience all day – and by the end of
the tour, while we looked spherical from all the waffles, they
all looked like Olympians from herding boxes all day.

The 'merch workout' – I'd buy the DVD.

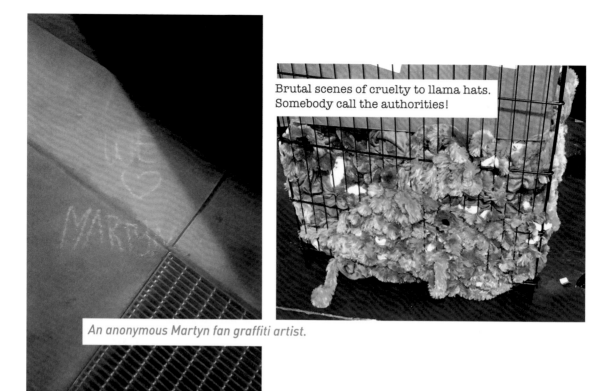

Brutal scenes of cruelty to llama hats. Somebody call the authorities!

An anonymous Martyn fan graffiti artist.

THE DESIGNS

We saw the tour as an opportunity to have some fun with the merch. The thing is that for most artists, the merch is 'cool' and edgy looking, usually because the artist is cool and edgy.

We're lame and soft, like pillows or slightly squashed marshmallows.

So, while usually with merch we try to think outside the box and it ends up being quite cute and colourful, with the tour we thought, "Hey, we're living the rock star dream, why not have rock star merch?!"

To be clear, we are joking.

Oh totally, it's completely ironic. We sought out a designer who'd drawn merch for actual bands that are actually rock 'n' roll and we said, "Hey, do it for Dan and Phil" – and thus:

TOTES EDGE.

And any coolness we've ever had just evaporated into a fine mist.

They're so cool looking, it's hilarious!

They are pretty funny. Then for America we had a conundrum: how can we change it to make the people of the USA like it?

Boom.

We apologise for nothing.

This is definitely one of those that I can't tell if it's more amazing or offensive?

Right in the middle, Phil, that's the sweet spot.

And what about Australia you ask? What colour tones and patterns speak to them?

indiscernible marsupial noises

It's basically sand and animal prints.

Australia!

All a true work of art. Dan and Phil, living the rock star dream,
one ironic t-shirt at a time.

Throughout this book you may have seen some truly scenic panoramas.

Sweeping vistas of beauty that give you unparalleled views of the world.

On this page you will find none of them.

This is a dark land for the panoramas that went horribly, horribly wrong.

What you see here may never be unseen, or forgiven.

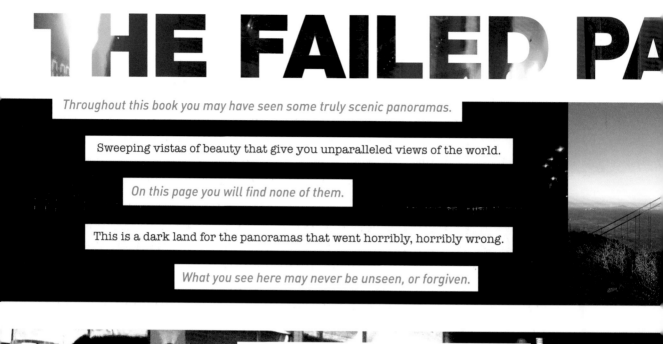

Okay you must have moved deliberately that time!

You're right; we knew what you were attempting.

Maybe the microwave was leaking radiation and the story of the show was about to come true?!

NORAMA ZONE

Nice idea. What a scenic background. But there seems to have been some kind of space/time implosion on the right there.

Alright, what happened in this theatre?

BURN IT. WHAT IS HAPPENING?

You were gesticulating about something and I didn't say I was taking it! Don't move during panoramas people.

STAGE TO SCREEN

Another huge thing we were working on while on tour (just keep adding to that pile) was the documentary film for YouTube Originals!

Planning this documentary, filming interviews for it and then planning the big show at the Dolby Theatre took up pretty much any free time we might have had!

It was crazy because we'd go from thinking about the tour, to making videos, to our cameraman, Matt, appearing out of thin air and going, "Surprise! Today is a filming day!" and we had to be ready to go.

Dan shamelessly styling himself.

The video gallery that was filming our performance at the Dolby! I was told not to go near it.

Yeah, before you immediately dropped that mirror and gave us all seven years of bad luck.

SRSBSNSS

I thought we all agreed I shouldn't be allowed to hold anything?! I blame everyone but me.

Dan having his true face attached.

CRAFTS

An important and beautiful part of our show was the crafts.

What is the Tumblr tag video series in real life, you ask? Well, it's the love child of Dan's old PO Box videos and DanAndPhilCRAFTS. A.K.A. a hellish dimension you will never erase from your memory.

Hey! I'd say only a strong half were inappropriate. There was a lot of genuinely great art in it too! Unfortunately, we could only pick six per show, but wading through people's creations was always a favourite part of my day.

Speaking of inappropriate, remember that sanitary pad with a derpy face of me stuck to it that someone named the 'Danitary Pad'?

That was a strong no from me and Director Ed. Thank all that is sacred that we are around to protect people's eyes.

Burn it.

A life-like sculpture of myself.

I don't see why you were so reluctant to wear this beautiful crown that was lovingly crafted for you.

You know cotton wool is one of my biggest fears! I almost imploded into a loose skin pile when you put that on my head.

The AmazingPhil furry fandom service, which nobody asked for.

Why?

Literally the most terrifying drawing ever created by humans. Thank you for scarring me!

Yes, that is a John Cena figure with a picture of Dil's face riding a Topiary llama.

I have been here since 2009 & will be here forever, changed my life for the better in so many ways and I can't thank you guys enough Love and hugs ♡

georgia
xoxox

IS THIS HAPPENING RIGHT NOW! #proud of yous ♡ so much ♡ phan and ♡ proud!
Phoebe
#O.TT

Hi Dan and Phil,
Thankyou for being the sunshines I need in life
Katie xxxx ♡

Name Tamara
Address Sydney, Australia.
Message Love you both so much!
thank you for radiating
happiness + positivity.
♡ Tamara

Welcome to Wales
remember to hug all dragons
heuh *rawr*

Thank-You for doing this tour! It was so surreal meeting you in Leeds!
Alisha
xoxo

To Dan & Phil
never stop doing
Youtube + Love sign

Why R U SO TALL?

Dear Dan & Phil, it's (som.. I ♡ you guys so much
Thank you for being born xx.
- Ceri-Anne. ♡

Name Marlee
Address amazing phil
Message

It's been really nice meeting you both! I hope I meet you again!

Faye

You brought my internet friends and I together, thank you!! ♡

Aly
I LOVE YOU SO MUCH EVEN YOU DAN

Thank you for everything! I'm never taking my light up flashy shoes off now! ♡ ABBIE xxx

To Dan & Phil
Thank-you for coming to Belfast :)
love you both. ♡
Victoria
x

Name Megan
Address
Message Thank you so much for coming to Texas! I met you at VidCon 2 years ago and you were just so great I had to see you again! I hope you have enjoyed America enough to want to come back again! Love you! ♡

Thanks for coming to glasgow got me two days off school. Apprantly I'm Dil! ☺liver
was going to draw/paint intricate portrait of you both as Pepe, but I didn't have the time nor energy
I am sorry.

I TRIED SO HARD

Hi!
Thank you for making this the best birthday ever! So proud of you!
love, Mia xxx

THINGS OVERHEARD ON TOUR!

Why does your bunk smell of peanut butter?

There is no fear greater than having a bee in your mouth.

How much whipped cream is too much whipped cream?

I got a Starbucks and they put my name as BONK.

Did you ever see a farmer put his hand up a cow when you were a kid?

Why is there a kettle in the shower?

Kalamawho?

I think I sat in a puddle of marmalade. At least I hope it was marmalade.

I saw a family of raccoons, so I knew it was important I called you.

Do you think blood will stain my dress?

I've always wanted to be a shepherd.

The Mummy Returns was underrated.

Do you think Chris Pratt is secretly attracted to his dinosaurs?

My abs are just squishier and less uptight.

Check your socks for scorpions! This is Texas after all.

Do you ever get a tingle when you remember there are ice-pops in the fridge?

Let me tweet a pic of your waffles! Mine look droopy.

Imagine if Spiderman got the face of a spider, would people still love him?

My hair looks like a squirrel mated with it.

I lost my glasses! Oh wait. They were on my head.

Don't come in! I'm slightly naked.

Make sure you label your suitcase in case the bus is hit by a tornado.

Has anyone seen my hair straighteners? This is a category 10 disaster.

That tasted like a mouthful of sand, but worse.

Someone buy me a maple syrup water pistol.

Sometimes it actually hurts me that I don't own a shibe.

HEY BOYS, YOU SMELL FRESH.

Do you think there are any undiscovered colours out there?

I fell out of my bed three times last night.

Are you having secret popcorn every night?

I wish I lived in the Bates Motel.

So, there we go. It happened. It was amazing, and thankfully at no point did anyone or anything get set on fire.

I don't think my career would have ever lived through the irony; we shouldn't tempt fate like that.

And here we are, sat back on the sofa in our apartment, looking at each other writing captions for a photo album.

It's really weird that we're making eye contact as we write this right now. I'd prefer it if you didn't make this meta – you're ruining everyone's immersion.

Sorry. What even is normal life like now that we're back? We've been on this train for so long I never even thought about what would happen when it stops.

I guess it's back to making videos and then contemplating whatever the future will be! Oh no, I enjoyed having a plan... Phil, what do I do now?!

Uh oh, Dan's gonna have a crisis. Don't worry; I'm sure you'll think of something soon (he's doomed). Just enjoy sleeping on a bed that isn't moving for days on end and not having to get dressed and interact with anyone.

Now that sounds like a Dan plan. I might just roleplay as a bear and hibernate.

This year has definitely been the craziest and best year of my life. When I was younger, I never would have even dreamed that what we've done is possible!

The fact that silly 'Dan and Phil' on YouTube somehow created this incredible community of friendship, support, creativity and happiness is by far what I'm proudest of in life.

We're just two guys that have fun trying to be entertaining. So to be able to go on this adventure and experience what we have is incredible and we're so grateful.

Plus, all the exercise this tour has given me has probably extended my life by 10 years, so that's good.

So, to everyone who supported us, thank you and may this lump of paper and ink preserve our memories forever.

zz zzz zz...

THAT'S A WRAP

For everyone around the world who came to see the show.

And everyone on the internet who's supported us for years.

Our incredible crew who helped us make the show.

Our squad that had to spend way too much time with us.

We actually did it. We went outside.

This was TATINOF...

Goodbye!